Human
Reproduction

Casey Rand

Raintree
Chicago, Illinois

www.heinemannraintree.com
Visit our website to find out
more information about
Heinemann-Raintree books.

To order:
☎ Phone 888-454-2279
🖥 Visit www.heinemannraintree.com
to browse our catalog and order online.

Edited by Adam Miller, Andrew Farrow, and
 Adrian Vigliano
Designed by Philippa Jenkins and Ken Vail
Original illustrations © Capstone Global Library
 Limited 2009
Illustrated by Ian Escott p5, 11, 16, 17, 22, 28;
 Maurizio De Angelis p9, 12, 13, 15, 27,30-31, 34
Picture research by Ruth Blair
Originated by Raintree
Printed and bound in China by South China Printing
 Company Ltd

13 12 11 10 09
10 9 8 7 6 5 4 3 2 1

Library of Congress Cataloging-in-Publication Data
Rand, Casey.
 Human reproduction / Casey Rand.
  p. cm. -- (Sci-hi. Life science)
 Includes bibliographical references and index.
 ISBN 978-1-4109-3327-0 (hc) -- ISBN 978-1-4109-
3335-5 (pb) 1. Human reproduction. I. Title.
 QP251.R36 2009
 612.6--dc22
                2009003464

Acknowledgments
The publishers would like to thank the following for
permission to reproduce copyright material: Corbis/
Clouds Hill Imaging Ltd. P. **7**, /Randy Faris pp. **23**, **40**,
/A. Inden/Zefa p. **6**, /Visuals Unlimited p. **20**, /Dennis
Wilson p. **19**, /Zhuoming Liang p. **39**; iStockphoto/
Ugur Evirgen pp. **3** (bottom), **21**; Photolibrary/age
fotostock p. **25**, /Brand X Pictures p. **37**, /Cusp p. **10**,
Science Photo Library p. **41**, John Bavosi p. **33**, BSIP,
BERANGER, p. **4**, Ian Hooton pp. **6**, **7**, KEITH/Custom
Medical Stock Photo p. **35**, Gary Parker pp. **3** (top), **29**;
Shutterstock: background images and design features.

Cover photo of fertilization used with permission of
Alamy/Stephen Sweet **main**. Cover image of newly
born babies and their mothers used with permission
of Alamy/Roger Bamber **inset**.

The publishers would like to thank literary consultant
Nancy Harris and content consultant Ann Fullick for
their assistance in the preparation of this book.

Every effort has been made to contact copyright
holders of any material reproduced in this book. Any
omissions will be rectified in subsequent printings if
notice is given to the publisher.

All the Internet addresses (URLs) given in this book
were valid at the time of going to press. However, due
to the dynamic nature of the Internet, some addresses
may have changed, or sites may have changed or
ceased to exist since publication. While the author and
Publishers regret any inconvenience this may cause
readers, no responsibility for any such changes can be
accepted by either the author or the Publishers.

Contents

Human Reproduction — 4

The Female Reproductive System — 8

The Male Reproductive System — 14

Fertilization: The Great Race — 18

DNA: The Human Library — 20

Union of Sperm and Egg — 24

Development in the Uterus — 30

Childbirth and the Newborn — 34

Growth and Development — 38

Timeline of Human Development and Life — 42

Amazing Facts — 44

Glossary — 45

Find Out More — 47

Index — 48

How are identical twins different than fraternal twins?

Go to page 29 to read why!

How is a cell's nucleus like a library?

Find out on page 21!

Some words are shown in bold, **like this**. These words are explained in the glossary. You will find important information and definitions underlined, <u>like this</u>.

HUMAN REPRODUCTION

What is human reproduction?

Human **reproduction** is the production of new humans. It is an amazing thing! <u>**A father and mother combine their own DNA (the material in all organisms that carries genetic information) to create a whole new person that is part of both of them.**</u> A pregnant mother carries the cellular beginnings of this new person inside of her for nine months. During these months the mother's body supplies the growing baby with food, liquid, and oxygen. How does it breathe inside its mother? Why do some babies look like their moms and others look like their dads? You will learn all this and more, so keep reading!

Thousands of babies are born everyday, all across the world!

Did you know?

Human reproduction is happening all the time all over the world. In fact, it is estimated that every day there are almost 350,000 new babies born in the world! That means that there are nearly 243 babies born every minute!

WHY REPRODUCE?

All species (types) of **organisms** (living things) must reproduce. All animals reproduce, and so do plants. <u>No matter how long an organism lives it will eventually die. In order for a species to survive, it must keep making new members.</u> Flies live for a very short time, so they must reproduce very quickly for the species to survive. Some trees, like the bristlecone pine, live for thousands of years! However, even these trees must reproduce so that their species will survive.

bristlecone pines
(1000—1500 years)

Giant tortoise
(150 years)

Human
(77 years)

Dog
(10—13 years)

Mouse
(4—6 months)

Each living thing is able to reproduce in a way that is best for the length of its life. Even though many insects, including flies, only live for a few days, they are very effective at reproducing!

Fly
(10—15 days)

THE CIRCLE OF LIFE

Each step involved in human reproduction has many interesting things to learn about. This book will introduce you to each of these steps.

5

Growth and maturation

The baby will continue to grow and mature until it becomes an adult and is ready to reproduce and begin the cycle again.

1 Reproduction

When adults determine that they are ready to have a baby they can begin the process of reproduction by having sexual intercourse. **Sexual intercourse allows a man and woman to mix their DNA together so a baby can be made.**

2 Fertilization

Once sexual intercourse has taken place, a **sperm** from the man can attach to an egg from the woman. **The cells from the sperm and egg contain all of the information (DNA) needed to make a new baby.**

3 Development

The fertilized egg grows, divides, and develops to form the new baby inside of the mother.

4 Childbirth

Eventually it is time for the mother's body to push the baby out into the world, to start growing on its own.

The Female Reproductive System

The parts of the body specially used for producing babies make up the **reproductive system**. The male and female reproductive systems are very different. Each is designed specifically for its purpose.

Internal fertilization

The human female is designed for internal **fertilization**. This means that a human mother keeps her eggs inside her body and carries her babies inside her body as well. <u>The female reproductive system makes and stores eggs. It allows these eggs to be fertilized by the male sperm.</u> Once fertilization takes place, this system feeds and protects the egg so that it can grow and eventually become a whole new person. Let's look at how the female is specially designed for this purpose.

Did you know?

The most children that one woman has given birth to in recent history is 69!! A Russian woman who lived in the 18th century gave birth to 16 sets of twins and 7 sets of quadruplets (4 babies at once) and a total of 69 babies in her lifetime!

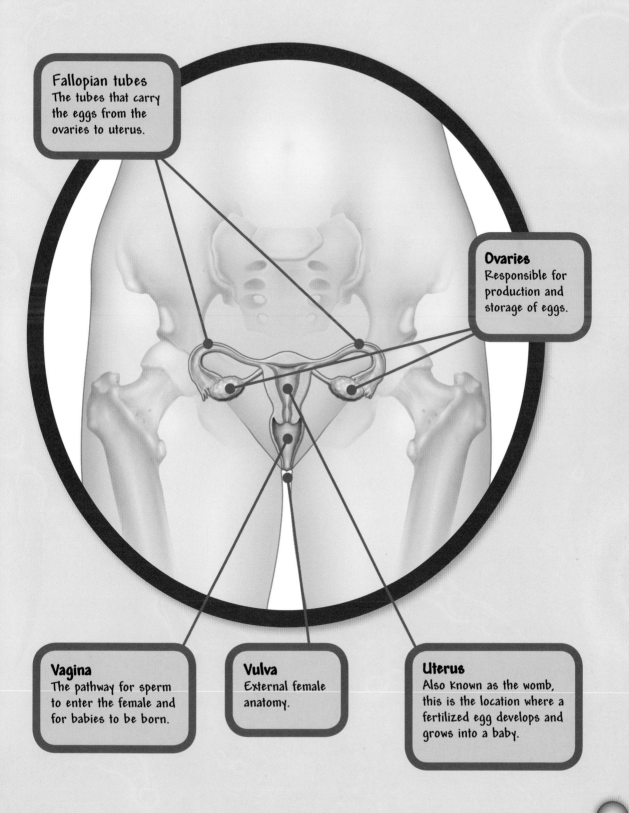

Fallopian tubes
The tubes that carry the eggs from the ovaries to uterus.

Ovaries
Responsible for production and storage of eggs.

Vagina
The pathway for sperm to enter the female and for babies to be born.

Vulva
External female anatomy.

Uterus
Also known as the womb, this is the location where a fertilized egg develops and grows into a baby.

Two incredible cells

Only two tiny cells are needed to begin a whole new life. The female reproductive system provides an egg as small as the period at the end of this sentence. The male reproductive system provides a sperm that is too small to see without a microscope. Under the right conditions these two tiny cells can work together to form each and every part of a new human being!

This girl looks like her mother because she grew from an egg cell from her mother, and a sperm cell from her father.

Ovaries

The female body makes and stores eggs in the ovaries. Before a female is born she has nearly 1 million eggs in each of her ovaries! These are all the eggs that the female will ever need. Inside the ovary, each egg is surrounded by a group of cells that is designed to protect and feed it. This group of cells is known as the **follicle**.

Egg anatomy

The egg is a specialized type of cell called an **oocyte**. Just like the other cells of the body the egg contains a **nucleus** (center of the cell) with DNA. It also has **cytoplasm**, the area surrounding the nucleus.

A healthy egg cell contains almost everything that is needed to begin developing into a new human—the process will begin if it is fertilized by a sperm cell.

nucleus

cytoplasm

follicle cells

Egg development

Ovulation usually begins in females between the ages of 11 and 13, though it could happen before or after this range. Ovulation is a process that happens every month, when a group of eggs in a female's ovaries gets ready to be fertilized and start the process of making a baby. Usually only one of the eggs completes this process. Once this egg is ready, the follicle pops and the egg is released from the ovary.

The female cycle

<u>**Approximately once each month the female reproductive system releases a ripe egg ready to be fertilized.**</u> Throughout the month several changes occur as the egg is prepared for fertilization. These changes happen regularly every month as long as the female is not pregnant. This cycle of changes is known as the **female cycle**, or **menstrual cycle**.

Hormones

The female cycle is controlled by **hormones**. Hormones are the messengers the body uses to send signals from one part of the body to another. The female cycle usually begins in girls between 11 and 13 years old. Once a female reaches this age her body releases specific hormones into her blood stream. These hormones tell the reproductive system to begin the cycle and prepare the egg and body for fertilization.

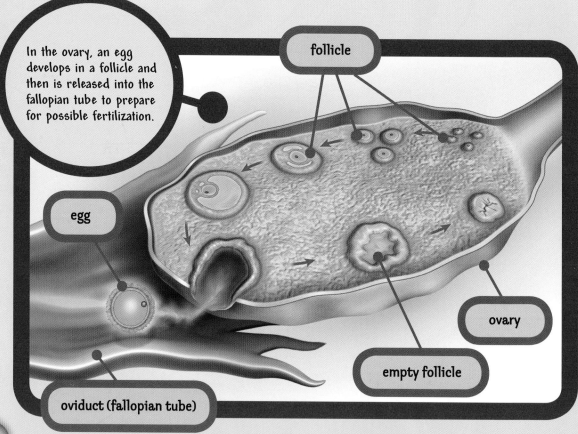

In the ovary, an egg develops in a follicle and then is released into the fallopian tube to prepare for possible fertilization.

follicle

egg

ovary

empty follicle

oviduct (fallopian tube)

When fertilization doesn't occur

If the egg is not fertilized at the end of the cycle, hormones tell the body that the changes it made to prepare for pregnancy are no longer needed. The lining of the uterus and the egg, along with some blood, is then washed out of the female's body. This is known as menstrual flow or a **period**. The cycle now ends and a new cycle begins.

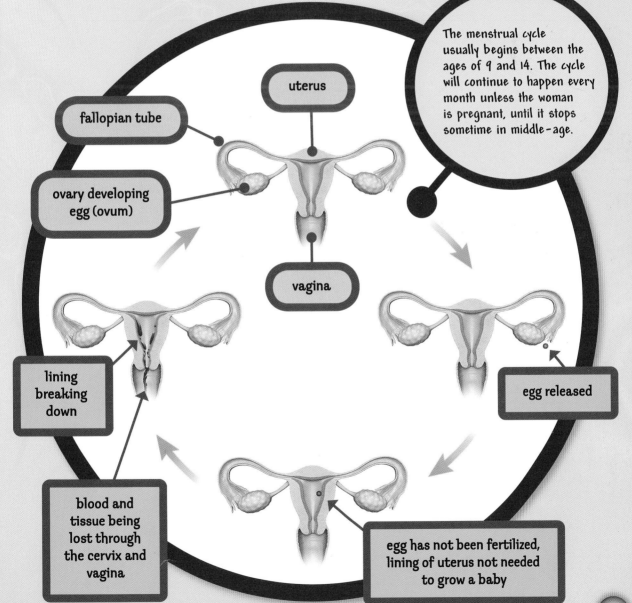

The menstrual cycle usually begins between the ages of 9 and 14. The cycle will continue to happen every month unless the woman is pregnant, until it stops sometime in middle-age.

fallopian tube

uterus

ovary developing egg (ovum)

vagina

lining breaking down

egg released

blood and tissue being lost through the cervix and vagina

egg has not been fertilized, lining of uterus not needed to grow a baby

The Male Reproductive System

Remember that it takes two special **cells** for a new baby to begin to develop. The first cell is the female egg. The second cell is the male **sperm**. The male reproductive system creates sperm in fluid called semen. <u>The male reproductive organ is designed to deposit this semen into the female so that fertilization can take place.</u>

Specialized designs

The male and female reproductive systems are very different from each other. Look at the different parts of each system. How is the female reproductive system specially designed for its purposes, internal fertilization and housing a developing baby? How is the male system differently designed for its own purposes, sperm production and fertilization of the female egg?

Did you know?

For sperm to develop and grow they must be kept at a temperature lower than normal body temperature. For this reason the male is specially adapted to hold the sperm outside of the body in the **testes** (testicles). It is possible to have a lower temperature here.

Seminal vesicle
Responsible for making fluid for semen.

Sperm duct
The tube that carries sperm away from the testes.

The male reproductive system is specially designed to work with the female reproductive system to fertilize the egg. Parts of the system also help to dispose of the body's liquid waste (urine).

Urethra
Thin tube that carries sperm and urine to the outside of the body through the penis.

Prostate gland
Responsible for making fluid for semen.

Penis
Used to deposit sperm inside the female vagina.

Epididymis
Tightly coiled tubes beside each of the testes where sperm mature and are stored.

Testes
Responsible for production and storage of sperm.

Sperm

Unlike the female eggs, which are formed before birth and stored throughout life, male sperm production begins in puberty and continues throughout adulthood. Everyday the average male produces over 300 million new sperm! Each of these sperm has the ability to fertilize a female egg and begin a new life.

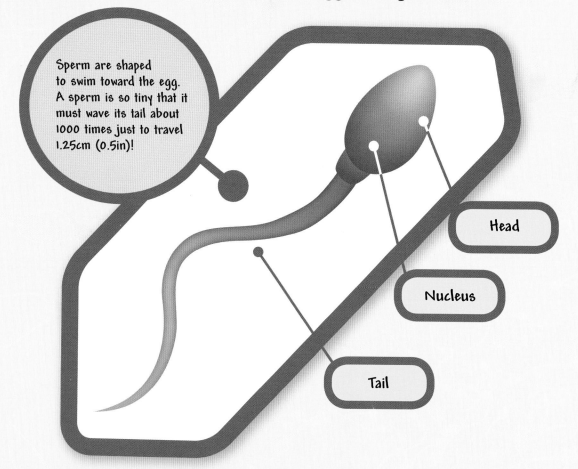

Sperm are shaped to swim toward the egg. A sperm is so tiny that it must wave its tail about 1000 times just to travel 1.25cm (0.5in)!

Head

Nucleus

Tail

Sperm production

The testes are responsible for producing the male sperm. Each of the testes is a ball made up of tiny tubes called **seminiferous tubules**. These tubes produce the tiny cells that will mature and become sperm. As the sperm cells mature they move into the epididymis (coiled tubes), where they will continue to mature (develop fully) and then be stored until needed. Eventually, if the sperm cells are not used, they will break down and new sperm cells will be made.

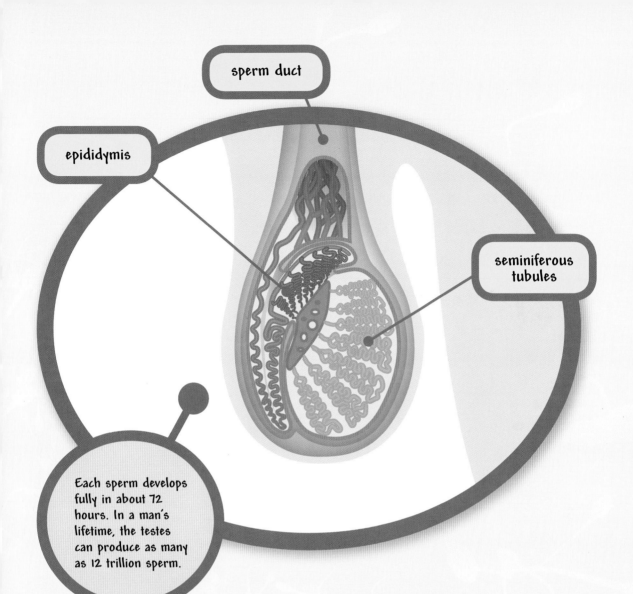

sperm duct

epididymis

seminiferous tubules

Each sperm develops fully in about 72 hours. In a man's lifetime, the testes can produce as many as 12 trillion sperm.

Anatomy of the sperm

A fully developed sperm cell resembles a tadpole but is thousands of times smaller. **__The head of the sperm cell contains half of the genetic material (DNA) that is needed to form the beginnings of a new person.__** The tail of the sperm is designed to help the sperm swim. The sperm must swim through the female reproductive tract to meet the egg.

Did you know?

Alcohol, drugs, and smoking all have very negative effects on sperm production. Males who smoke may only produce half of the sperm of other males.

Fertilization: The Great Race

In order for fertilization to occur, sperm must be deposited in the female during sexual intercourse. Then the sperm races through the female reproductive tract, to meet the egg. Let's look at how both the reproductive systems work to bring the egg and sperm together.

The pathway of the egg

Each month a single egg develops and is released from the **ovary** as discussed on page 11. The mature egg then moves to the **oviduct** into position to meet the sperm. The oviduct is a tube where the eggs pass from the ovary.

The pathway of sperm

The **penis** fills with blood and becomes erect to make sexual intercourse possible. During intercourse, the muscles around the penis push sperm into the female **vagina**. 300-500 million sperm may enter the vagina at once! **In the reproductive tract the sperm race toward the uterus to meet the egg.** The sperm must swim from the vagina, through the uterus, and into the oviducts. The sperm are pushed along by their tails.

Did you know?

Sperm must swim nearly 20 cm (8 in) once inside the vagina. This may not seem like a long distance but 20 cm (8 in) is nearly 5,000 times the length of the average sperm. This is the same as a 1.5 m (5 ft) tall person swimming nearly 8 km (5 miles)!

And the winner is....

Even though millions of sperm may enter the vagina at one
time, only one sperm can fertilize the egg. That means that out
of 300 million sperm racing to the female egg, there is only one
that can join with the egg. The sperm that helped make you had
to beat out millions of other sperm just to be a part of you!

DNA: The Human Library

We have seen that for **fertilization** to occur the **sperm and egg** must join to become one. But how do these two little **cells** know what to do once they combine? How do they go from sperm and egg, to a breathing, moving, and crying baby in only 9 months? The answer is DNA.

What is DNA?

<u>**DNA is a chemical which carries the instructions that tell a cell how to build a whole new person.**</u> The DNA tells some cells to become blood, some cells to become hair, and some cells to become skin. DNA contains all of this information!

DNA is made up of four bases that scientists call **nucleotides**. Scientists use the letters A, G, C, and T to represent the four bases of DNA. These bases are like the letters of the alphabet. You already know that letters of the alphabet combine to form sentences. In a similar way the bases of DNA combine to form sequences called **genes**. Genes tell the cell to make certain types of **proteins**. These proteins are the structures that help cells become specialized as blood, hair, skin, or other parts of the body.

Here you can see chromosomes inside a human cell. The blob at the bottom is the cell nucleus.

CHROMOSOMES

In each cell there are over 3 billion nucleotides (basic units of DNA) of DNA sequence! How do the tiny cells hold so much DNA? <u>DNA is organized and packaged into structures called **chromosomes**.</u> Chromosomes are like books that are used to organize the DNA. Human beings contain 46 chromosomes in each of their cells. These chromosomes are all stored in a special area of the cell called the **nucleus**. It's like each cell has a library called the nucleus with 46 books called chromosomes. This library contains all of the information needed to make each and every part of a human being.

Most living things have chromosomes, but in many different numbers. Potatoes have 48, dogs have 78, and the adder's tongue fern plant has 1,440!

HUMAN CHROMOSOME VOL. 16

HUMAN CHROMOSOME VOL. 15

HUMAN CHROMOSOME VOL. 14

HUMAN CHROMOSOME VOL. 13

HUMAN CHROMOSOME VOL. 12

HUMAN CHROMOSOME VOL. 11

HUMAN CHROMOSOME VOL. 10

HUMAN CHROMOSOME VOL. 9

HUMAN CHROMOSOME VOL. 8

HUMAN CHROMOSOME VOL. 7

HUMAN CHROMOSOME VOL. 6

HUMAN CHROMOSOME VOL. 4

HUMAN CHROMOSOME VOL. 3

Heredity

You may have heard that you have the "same" nose as your father or eyes just like your mom. So how did your father's nose or mother's eyes get on your face? The answer is **heredity**. <u>Heredity is the passing of traits, like nose shape and eye color, from one generation to the next.</u> Read on to find out more.

DNA in the egg and sperm

The egg and sperm are special cells with unique features designed specifically for **reproduction**. One unique feature of these cells is that each contains only half of the DNA that other cells contain. That is, there are only 23 DNA books, or chromosomes, in the library of the sperm and egg. These cells each contain only half the DNA of normal cells because they combine to form the beginnings of a new person.

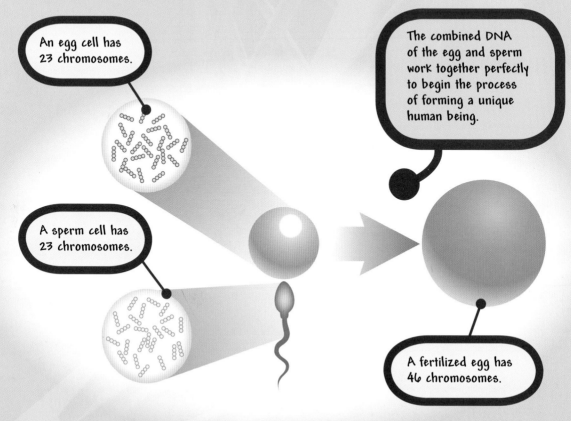

An egg cell has 23 chromosomes.

The combined DNA of the egg and sperm work together perfectly to begin the process of forming a unique human being.

A sperm cell has 23 chromosomes.

A fertilized egg has 46 chromosomes.

From parents to children

Although the DNA sequence of all humans is similar, no one's DNA sequence is exactly like another person's. This is why every person looks unique. Remember that DNA tells our cells how to grow and look. So differences in DNA sequence cause the cells in one person to grow and look differently than those in another person. The cells that become a new baby get their DNA from the father's sperm and mother's egg. Since DNA is passed down from parents to children, parents can also pass down the traits that their DNA tells their cells to make, like blue eyes or blonde hair.

> The members of a family may look very similar, or not very similar at all! Everyone's combination of DNA is unique.

You are unique

Each sperm or egg contains half of the DNA of the father or mother. However, each time a sperm or egg is made it has a unique combination of DNA. The chromosomes mix and recombine differently in every cell. This is why brothers and sisters may look similar but not the same. Each received half of their DNA from their mother and half from their father, but the DNA they each received has a unique combination.

Union of Sperm and Egg

When a **sperm cell** reaches the female egg, **fertilization** occurs. During this process the two cells become one, bringing together **DNA** from the man and the woman. <u>The new cell contains an entire library of 46 **chromosomes**, all of the information necessary for a new baby to form.</u> So what exactly happens when the sperm gets to the egg?

Sperm and egg combine

When a sperm reaches the egg, it pushes its head into the egg. This joins the lining of the egg and the sperm together. Now the 23 chromosomes from the sperm can join the 23 chromosomes from the egg. The female egg immediately begins to form a thick barrier that other sperm cells cannot break through. This ensures that the egg is only fertilized by one sperm cell and the correct amount of chromosomes, 46, remains in the fertilized egg.

POPULATION EXPLOSION!

The process of fertilization, pregnancy, and birth is very long and highly complex. Even so, the human race is reproducing at a very successful rate. As of September 2008, the world's population is estimated to be over 6.7 billion people! If human reproduction continues at its current rate, the world's population will reach 9 billion by 2042!

Homunculus

Before technology allowed for the discovery of DNA, there were several theories about how babies were formed. One of the most interesting of these theories was the Homunculus theory. This theory was popular in the 17th century. At the time, many scientists believed that the female egg or male sperm actually held a fully formed, tiny person inside of them. So a mother or father would carry this very small person inside of them at all times. They also believed that this small person held another, even smaller person inside of them, who held another inside of them, and so on. In fact they believed that every human that would ever live was already formed, living inside of someone else, waiting to be born!

The Homunculus theory was something like these Russian dolls. The theory guessed that each small person carried a smaller person inside.

The fertilized egg

__After the egg and sperm have combined, the new cell immediately begins the development that will end in the formation of a new baby.__ But how does a single cell become an entire human being? Read on to find out more.

From oviduct to implantation

The sperm normally meets the egg in the **oviduct** just outside of the female **ovaries**. However, the egg must move into the **uterus**, where it will implant (attach) itself in the wall. This is called implantation. The time from fertilization to implantation is normally four to five days.

Cleavage

As the fertilized egg travels toward the uterus it undergoes several divisions as seen in the picture at right. These divisions are known as **cleavage**. After only 36 hours, the fertilized egg splits into two cells and the divisions continue approximately every 12 hours until implantation. The new cells remain together in one ball called a **zygote**. As the cells enter the uterus they form a ball of around 50–80 cells.

Implantation

The zygote must now attach itself to the lining of the wall of the uterus. This lining is called the **endometrium**. When the zygote attaches to the endometrium it signals the female body to stop the **menstrual cycle**. This is why a pregnant female will not have menstrual flow.

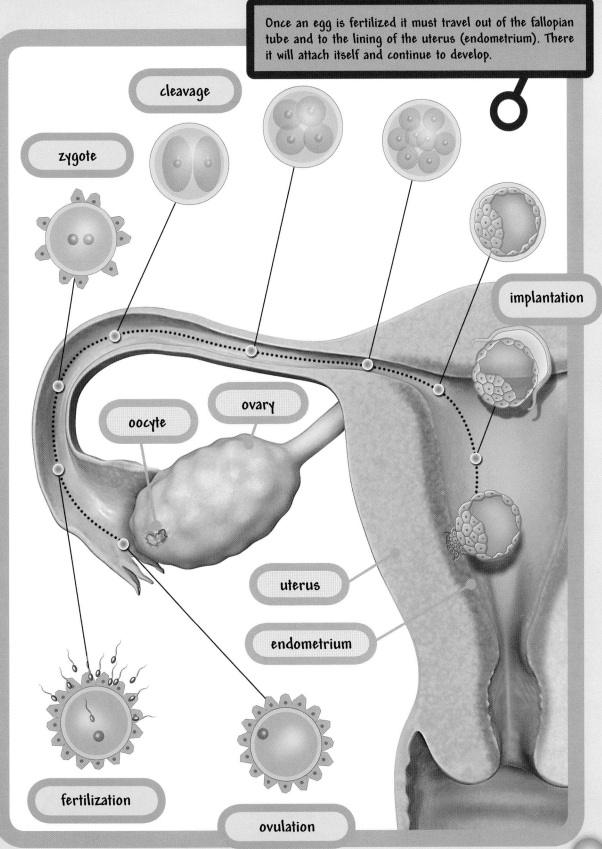

Once an egg is fertilized it must travel out of the fallopian tube and to the lining of the uterus (endometrium). There it will attach itself and continue to develop.

cleavage

zygote

implantation

oocyte

ovary

uterus

endometrium

fertilization

ovulation

Twins, triplets, and beyond

Usually one sperm fertilizes one egg and one new baby develops. However there are special circumstances in which a female may become pregnant with 2 or more babies at once. Does this mean that 2 eggs were fertilized by two different sperm? Or that more than one sperm fertilized one egg? Here are three things that can happen.

It is possible for 2 or more eggs to be released in a menstrual cycle. Once eggs have been released, it is possible for all of them to be fertilized.

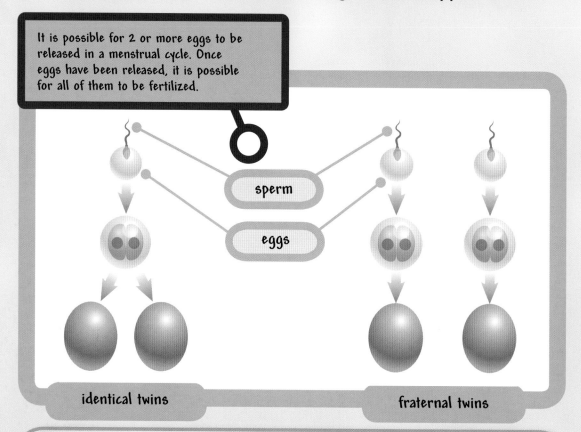

sperm

eggs

identical twins

fraternal twins

Fraternal twins

Sometimes a female will release more than one egg in one menstrual cycle. In this situation both eggs may be fertilized by different sperm. These are called **fraternal twins**. These twins will look no more alike than any other siblings. Remember that each egg and sperm carries a unique combination of DNA. Since each of these twins is formed from a different egg and a different sperm, they will each have a different combination of DNA. They may or may not be the same gender.

These girls are identical twins. This means that their DNA first combined inside of one egg before splitting in two.

Identical twins

Identical twins are both formed from the same egg and the same sperm. This is a very special situation in which a fertilized egg divides and forms two different zygotes or balls of cells. Each of these balls of cells will grow into a new baby with almost the exact same combination of DNA. That is why these twins will look so much alike. Identical twins always share the same gender (female or male).

Triplets and beyond

Sometimes a mother can become pregnant with even more than two babies at once. This can result from either of the situations already listed or through some combination of both. In the case of quadruplets (four babies in the uterus at once) for instance, it is possible that there will be one set of fraternal twins and one set of identical twins.

Development in the Uterus

After the **zygote** attaches to the lining of the **uterus** the **cells** of the zygote begin to **differentiate**. This means that the cells start to become specialized for the different parts of the baby they will become. This is known as the **embryonic** stage of development. It lasts for eight weeks. <u>**During this period cells start to form the main systems of the body including the heart, nerves, stomach, brain, muscles, and skin.**</u> The embryo starts to take shape and look like a human baby.

For humans, pregnancy lasts for about nine months. However, the amount of development that happens during that time is incredible!

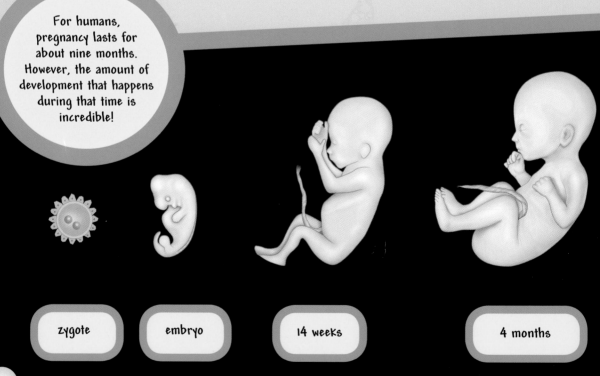

| zygote | embryo | 14 weeks | 4 months |

Fetal development

Once the embryo has taken shape, the fetal period of development begins. This period will last from about nine weeks until the baby is born. At this point the major systems and structures of the baby have already developed. The body continues to grow at a rapid pace, getting ready to move to the outside world. Also, the more detailed features of the body form during this period. For instance the nose, lips, and facial structures develop, and hair begins to grow on the baby's head.

Did you know?

Although the female reproductive system is designed to carry only one offspring at a time it has been known to carry many more. Recently, with the widespread use of **fertility drugs** designed to make becoming pregnant more likely, multiple births have become more frequent. In fact a couple in Texas recently gave birth to octuplets!! That is 8 babies at once! Imagine all of the diapers.

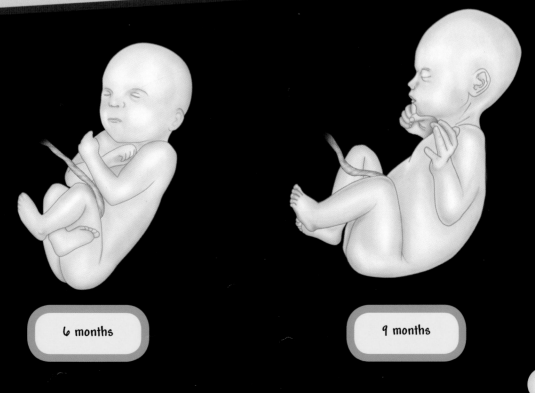

6 months

9 months

Fetal nourishment

As the fetus grows it requires **nutrients** (nutrition from food sources) and oxygen, just as it will after being born. But how does the growing fetus get what it needs?

The placenta

Some of the same cells that develop from the fertilized egg and sperm to become the fetus, also form a structure called the **placenta**. The placenta is connected to the fetus by the **umbilical cord**. The umbilical cord is a tube connecting the placenta to the navel (belly button) of the fetus. <u>The purpose of the placenta is to allow the transfer of nutrients and oxygen from the mother to the fetus. This is done through the umbilical cord.</u> The placenta also transfers waste products from the fetus back to the mother for disposal from the body.

Amniotic fluid

The growing fetus is supported and protected by a pool of liquid known as **amniotic fluid**. This liquid contains substances important for the fetus' growth and development. The fluid also acts as a cushion that absorbs the shock of any bumps or fast movements.

Did you know?

When a pregnant mother smokes, her baby smokes, too. The same poisons that enter a mother's lungs while smoking enter the placenta and baby. Smoking increases the risk of **premature** (born before fully ready) and low birth-weight babies being born. This can cause disabilities such as learning problems. It also increases the risk that the baby will die just before or after birth.

The effects of a mother's choices

A developing fetus must breathe, drink, and eat what his or her mother breathes, drinks, and eats. This is why a mother's diet and lifestyle choices are so important to a baby's development. While inside the mother, the baby's body grows faster than it will ever grow again. The baby needs vitamins and nutrients to maintain this growth. The baby needs to avoid drugs, alcohol, and smoking to develop correctly. All of these things can transfer through the placenta to the baby and have horrible consequences.

Before being born a baby takes up a large amount of space in its mother's body. At birth, most babies weigh between 6 and 9 pounds.

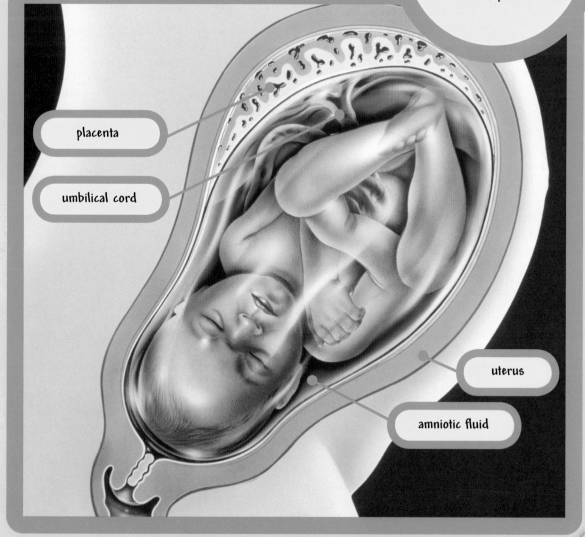

placenta

umbilical cord

uterus

amniotic fluid

Childbirth and the Newborn

After a certain period of time developing in the mother's womb, usually close to nine months, the baby is ready to leave the womb and enter the world. The muscles of the **uterus** begin to contract regularly to squeeze the baby out of the mother's body. The process by which a baby is born is called "labor" because it is very hard work!

Contractions

Contractions are the rhythmic squeezing of the muscles of the mother's uterus. Usually, once the contractions get going, the mother's "water breaks." This means the **amniotic fluid** that has been surrounding and protecting the baby is released. The contractions get closer together, longer and stronger as labor progresses. They can be very painful. The contractions push the baby through the **cervix** and out through the **vagina**. The baby usually moves head first out into the world.

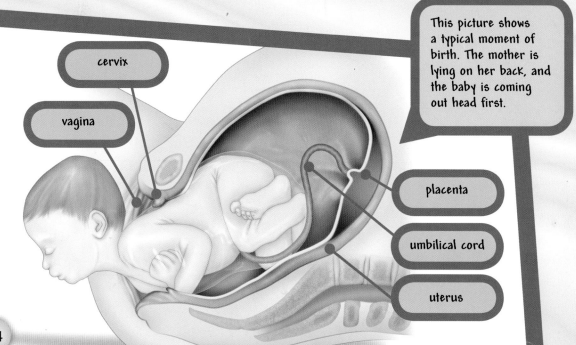

cervix

vagina

This picture shows a typical moment of birth. The mother is lying on her back, and the baby is coming out head first.

placenta

umbilical cord

uterus

The placenta

Once the baby is out of the mother, the **placenta** must be pushed out as well. Contractions continue until the placenta as well as other skin and fluids that the mother no longer needs are pushed out.

The baby

As soon as the baby is born it will usually cry loudly. This is the first time the baby's lungs have had to breathe air on their own, so this step is important. The **umbilical cord** will now be clamped off and cut so that the baby's system can take over completely.

Did you know?

The average newborn baby weighs around 3.2 kg (7 lbs). However some babies are much bigger or smaller. The largest baby recorded weighed over 11 kg (23 lbs). This is more than three times the size of the average baby!

This baby has just been born. The gray-colored umbilical cord is still attached to the baby.

The newborn

The newborn period, right after a baby is born, is very important. **The human baby is very dependent on others and special care is needed.**

Bonding

After birth the baby gets to know its parents or those caring for it. The baby quickly learns to recognize familiar voices and even the smell of its mother. Newborn babies are nearsighted. This means that they can only see 20 to 30 cm (8 to 12 inches) away, so sound and smell are very important.

Newborn nourishment

The mammary glands of a mother produce milk for the newborn after birth. This is not like the milk that we buy at the grocery store. It contains special nutrients for human growth. It also contains antibodies to protect the baby against sickness until its own systems can develop further.

Newborn facts!

- Newborns sleep 15-20 hours every day.

- Newborn babies cry a lot, but actually don't produce any tears.

- A newborn's heart beats 130 to 160 times per minute, that is nearly twice as fast as your heart beats!

A newborn gets to know his or her family through touch, smell, sound, and sight.

Growth and Development

During infancy and childhood, growth and development continue at a rapid pace. What periods are the most important in a child's growth?

Infancy

Babies continue to develop quickly during the first year of life. This period is known as infancy. At this point the baby's head makes up almost 25 percent of its weight. The baby's brain develops more quickly than other body parts. This allows a baby to learn quickly. In the first year of life a baby may learn to smile, play, eat, and begin to recognize and use language. This is also the fastest growth period of a human's life. During this single year the baby will nearly triple its weight!

Childhood

After the first year of life the baby enters a period especially important to learning. This time is called childhood. Physical growth during childhood continues, although at a slower pace than during infancy. The child will also begin to develop more advanced language skills. This may include the beginning of writing and reading as well as increasing spoken vocabulary.

Get a grip!

Babies are born with a strong grasping reflex. From birth they can grasp so tightly that they can even support their own weight for a few moments! As their hands develop, grasping becomes less of a reflex. Before long, they learn how to do things like grip a spoon—or drop toys down the stairs!

During the first year of life, the infant grows and develops faster than any other time in life.

How and why we grow

The body grows because of an increase in the size and number of its cells. Just like during early **embryonic development**, the cells of the body continue to divide and grow during this period. The way a child grows and develops is a result of the genes the child inherited from its parents. Remember that these genes are the instructions that tell the body how to grow and develop.

Did you know?

Tiger Woods began to play golf at two years of age.

Mozart began composing music at five years of age.

Puberty and beyond

As a young person grows older, they enter a period of growth and development that will prepare their bodies to start the cycle of human **reproduction** over again. <u>**Puberty is a time period when the body's reproductive organs begin to develop and mature.**</u> This period is very different for boys and girls.

Male development

Puberty begins for most boys between the ages of 12 and 14 years. It may begin with a rapid period of physical growth. During this time the male body begins to produce large amounts of the hormone **testosterone**. This hormone controls many of the changes that take place during this period. These changes include rapid growth, development of muscles, and growth of the reproductive organs. They also include deepening of the voice, growth of pubic hair, and production of **semen**.

For most boys, puberty can begin anywhere between ages 9 and 14. The process is usually complete by age 18.

Adulthood

After puberty is over the body will remain relatively stable, that is not growing or dramatically changing, throughout the rest of the lifetime. The body is now fully capable of reproducing and the human life cycle can start again. The fertilized egg has grown from a single cell into a fully grown human being.

Female development

Puberty begins for most girls between the ages of 10 and 12, and may also begin with a period of rapid physical growth. During this time the female will begin to produce large amounts of the hormones **estrogen** and **progesterone**. Like testosterone in the male, estrogen and progesterone control many of the changes and developments in the female body during this time. These hormones control the development of rapid growth, pubic hair, breasts and reproductive organs, and the start of the **menstrual cycle**.

For most girls puberty can begin anywhere between ages 8 and 12. Puberty for girls can be over as early as age 12 or even as late as 19.

TIMELINE OF HUMAN DEVELOPMENT AND LIFE

From the moment a tiny sperm cell attaches to the female egg an amazing journey begins. This journey will change the tiny cells into a living, breathing human. Let's take a look at some of the steps along the way.

Day 1	Fertilization occurs, DNA from the mother and father combine.
Days 7 to 14	Cells multiply and become specialized for muscle, bone, and other functions.
Day 22	Heart begins to beat.
Week 4	Skeleton forms and muscles develop; arms and legs begin to form.
Week 7	Can kick and move.
Week 8	Can begin to hear.
Weeks 9 and 10	Can turn its head, make facial expressions, and hiccup.
Week 18	All structures are now completely formed needing only more time to grow.
Months 5 and 6	The baby practices breathing and is 30 cm (12 inches) long or more and can weigh up to 0.7 kg (1.5 pounds).
Months 7 through 9	The baby is using four of the five senses (vision, hearing, taste, and touch).

Birth

1 month	The baby can lift its head a little when lying on stomach and watch objects for a short time.
3 months	The baby can recognize bottle or breast, as well as a familiar smile.
6 months	The baby can respond to a friendly voice with a smile or coo.
9 months	The baby can say "mama" and "dada" and crawl.
12 months	The baby can stand and may step with support.
2 years	The baby can use two or three words together and potty training begins.
4 years	The child begins to learn how to read.
6 years	The child starts school.
10 to 13 years	Puberty begins.

Amazing Facts

Amazing facts about the reproductive system

◆ The largest cell in the human body is the female egg. The smallest is the male sperm.

Amazing facts about heredity

◆ Everyone has a unique smell, except for identical twins. This is because our smell is partly determined by our genes!

◆ The characteristic for having dimples is dominant over the characteristic for no dimples. So if you get a dimple gene from your mom and a no-dimple gene from your dad, you will end up with at least one dimple!

Amazing facts about the zygote

◆ At one point in development every human consisted of just one single, tiny cell!

◆ Your body now consists of around 100 trillion cells!

Amazing facts about fetal development

◆ A fetus' teeth start growing almost six months before the baby is even born!

◆ A fetus acquires fingerprints at the age of three months!

Amazing facts about childbirth

◆ Of every 2,000 newborns, only one will have a tooth when it is born!

◆ Scientists estimate that human babies are, pound for pound, stronger than an ox. This means that if a seven pound baby was the same size as an ox, the baby would be stronger!

Amazing facts about growth and development

◆ From birth, a human's eyes are always the same size.

◆ A human's nose and ears never stop growing!

◆ Only 7 percent of the people on Earth are left-handed!

Glossary

amniotic fluid pool of liquid inside the uterus that protects and nourishes the developing baby

cell smallest functioning unit of an organism

cervix narrow end of the uterus that opens into the vagina

chromosomes bodies in the nucleus of the cell that contain and organize DNA

cleavage dividing of cells that helps the sperm and egg become the different parts of the body

contraceptive method or device that prevents pregnancy from beginning

contraction rhythmic squeezing of the muscles of the mother's uterus. Contractions help push the baby out of the mother's body.

cytoplasm material in a cell that is not the nucleus

differentiate to become different

DNA material in living creatures that carries genetic information. DNA is contained in chromosomes.

embryo developing ball of cells after it has implanted in the uterus

embryonic development process by which an embryo develops

endometrium lining of the uterus

epididymis male reproductive gland that is composed of coiled tubes which store sperm

estrogen one of the primary female sex hormones

female cycle (See *menstrual cycle*)

fertility drugs medicines that make pregnancy more likely

fertilization union of the male sperm and female egg to form the zygote

fetal development process by which a fetus develops

follicle round structure in the female ovary that is made of one egg and the cells that surround and protect it

fraternal twins twins formed when two eggs are fertilized by two sperm. These twins are not identical.

gene stretch of DNA located on a chromosome that tells a cell to make a specific protein

heredity the passing of traits from one generation to the next

hormones messengers that body parts release into the bloodstream to communicate with other body parts

identical twins twins formed from one egg and one sperm

mammary gland glands responsible for milk production in the female

menstrual cycle the female cycle responsible for preparing an egg for fertilization

nucleotide basic unit of DNA

nucleus central part of a cell. The nucleus contains the cell's genetic material.

nutrient substance that provides the nourishment that is needed for life

oocyte immature female egg

organism individual living thing

ovary organ in the body of females that produces and stores eggs

oviduct tube in the female for the passage of eggs from the ovary

ovulation process that releases eggs from the ovaries

penis male reproductive organ through which semen is carried into the female during intercourse

period end of the menstrual cycle where the female body washes the unused egg, lining, and some blood out of the body

placenta organ that joins the developing baby to the uterus and aids in fetal nutrition

premature when something happens too early

progesterone one of the primary female sex hormones

protein structures created by genes that help cells of the body specialize

reflex action taken by our bodies automatically, often in response to something

reproduction to generate offspring by sexual or asexual means

reproductive system parts of the body specifically used for producing babies

semen fluid produced by the male reproductive system that contains sperm

seminal vesicle tubes that carry sperm away from the testes toward the penis

seminiferous tubules tubes inside the testes that are responsible for sperm production

sperm cell produced by the male reproductive system that is capable of fertilizing the female egg

testes male reproductive gland that produces sperm

testosterone primary male sex hormone

umbilical cord tube which carries nutrients and oxygen to a developing baby. It also takes waste away.

urethra tube that runs inside penis and carries semen, as well as urine, out of the male body

uterus muscular organ of a female in which the baby develops before birth. It is also known as the womb.

vagina canal where sperm enters the female body and a baby exits

vulva part of the female reproductive system that is outside the body

zygote cell formed by the union of the egg and sperm. The zygote lasts for about four days before developing further.

Find Out More

Books

Brynie, Faith Hickman. ***101 Questions About Sex and Sexuality: With Answers for the Curious, Cautious, and Confused***. Minneapolis, MN: Twenty-first Century Books, 2003.

Parker, Steve. ***In Your Genes: Genetics and Reproduction***. Chicago: Raintree, 2007.

Snedden, Robert. ***Cell Division and Genetics***. New York: Rosen 2009.

Traugh, Susan M. ***Sex Smarts: You and Your Sexuality***. Mankato, MN: Compass Point, 2009.

Websites

http://www.innerbody.com/htm/body.html
An interactive tour of the male and female reproductive systems.

http://learn.genetics.utah.edu/content/begin/traits/index.html
An interactive walk through inheritance.

http://www.usoe.k12.ut.us/curr/science/sciber00/7th/genetics/sciber/intro.htm
A fun site on reproduction and heredity.

http://www.sciencenewsforkids.org/
Lots of interesting science designed just for kids.

http://www.extremescience.com/index.html
A site with some of the most unbelievable scientific facts.

http://www.units.muohio.edu/dragonfly/family/index.shtml
A site that explains heredity. Find out why you look like you do.

Index

adulthood 6, 7, 16, 41
amniotic fluid 32, 33, 34
antibodies 36

bases 20
birth 4, 6, 31, 34, 35
birth weight 35
bonding 36
breasts 9, 41

cervix 13, 34
childhood 38
chromosomes 21, 22, 23, 24
chromosomes diagram 22
cleavage 26, 27
cleavage diagram 27
contraceptives 13
contractions 34, 35
cytoplasm 11

deaths 5, 32, 37
differentiation 30
DNA 4, 7, 11, 17, 20, 21, 22, 23, 24, 25, 28

egg diagram 11
eggs 6, 7, 8, 9, 10, 11, 12, 13, 14, 16, 17, 18, 19, 22, 23, 24, 25, 26, 28, 29, 32, 37, 41
embryonic stage 30
endometrium 26, 27
epididymis 15, 16, 17
estrogen 41

fallopian tubes 9, 13
female cycle (See menstrual cycle)
female reproductive diagram 9
female reproductive system 8, 9, 10, 11, 12, 13
fertility drugs 31
fertilization 6, 19, 20, 24, 27, 28
fertilization diagram 22
fetal stage 31, 32, 33
fetal stage diagram 33
follicle 10, 11, 12
fraternal twins 28, 29
fraternal twins diagram 28

genes 20, 39
grasping reflex 38

heredity 22
Homunculus theory 25
hormones 12, 13, 40, 41

identical twins 29
identical twins diagram 28
implantation 26, 27
implantation diagram 27
infancy 38
internal fertilization 8

language skills 38

male reproductive diagram 15
male reproductive system 14, 15, 16, 17
mammary glands 36
menstrual cycle 12, 26, 41
menstrual cycle diagram 12
menstrual flow 13
menstrual flow diagram 13

nearsightedness 36
newborns 35, 36
nucleotides 20, 21
nucleus 11, 16, 21
nutrients 32, 33, 36

octuplets 31
oocyte cells 11, 27
ovaries 9, 10, 11, 12, 13, 18, 26, 27
oviducts 12, 18, 26
ovulation 11, 27

penis 15, 18
period (See menstrual flow)
placenta 32, 33, 35
population 24
progesterone 41
prostate gland 15
proteins 20
puberty 16, 40, 41

quadruplets 29

reproductive tract 17, 18

semen 14, 40
seminal vesicle 15
seminiferous tubules 16, 17
sexual intercourse 7, 18
specialized cells 20, 30
sperm 7, 8, 10, 14, 15, 16, 17, 18, 19, 22, 23, 24, 25, 26, 28, 29, 32
sperm cell diagram 16
sperm ducts 15, 17
substance abuse 17, 32, 33

temperature 14
termites 37
testes 14, 15, 16, 17
testes diagram 17
testosterone 40
timeline 42–43
traits 22, 23
triplets 29
twins 28, 29
twins diagrams 28

umbilical cord 32, 35
urethra 15
uterus 9, 13, 18, 26, 27, 30, 33, 34

vagina 9, 13, 18, 19, 34
vulva 9

zygotes 26, 27, 29, 30